and so to bed: 25 dreamy bed-dressing ideas

sleep on it

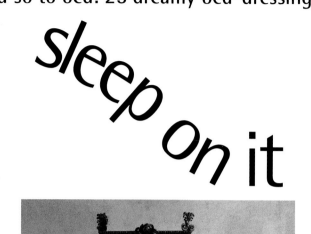

Stewart and Sally Walton

southwater

747.77

This edition is published by Southwater

Distributed in the UK by
The Manning Partnership
251–253 London Road East
Batheaston
Bath BA1 7RL
tel. 01225 852 727
fax 01225 852 852

Published in the USA by
Anness Publishing Inc.
27 West 20th Street
Suite 504
New York
NY 10011
fax 212 807 6813

Distributed in Canada by
General Publishing
895 Don Mills Road
400–402 Park Centre
Toronto, Ontario M3C 1W3
tel. 416 445 3333
fax 416 445 5991

Distributed in Australia by
Sandstone Publishing
Unit 1, 360 Norton Street
Leichhardt
New South Wales 2040
tel. 02 9560 7888
fax 02 9560 7488

Southwater is an imprint of Anness Publishing Limited
Hermes House, 88–89 Blackfriars Road, London SE1 8HA
tel. 020 7401 2077; fax 020 7633 9499

© Anness Publishing Limited 1996, 2002

Publisher: Joanna Lorenz
Senior Editor: Lindsay Porter
Assistant Editor: Sarah Ainley
Photographer: Graham Rae
Stylist: Catherine Tully
Designer: Caroline Reeves

Previously published as *Bed Dressing*

1 3 5 7 9 10 8 6 4 2

CONTENTS

INTRODUCTION

If you don't know a four-poster from a half-tester, or have always fancied a futon but didn't know

what to put on it, then this book is for you. This is spontaneous and creative interior design for

people who don't want to play by the rules. There are 25 different ideas for dressing up basic beds

and transforming them into sleeping quarters of style and distinction. Each one has its own

individual personality and there really is something for everyone.

None of the projects require you to have advanced DIY or soft-furnishing skills but they do promise

dramatic transformations if you are willing to have a go. Tools and special equipment have been kept

to a minimum – the only two indispensable items are a staple gun and a glue gun. These two tools

provide freedom from conventional methods of construction, fixing and draping, and allow you to

achieve the impossible – and keep it there.

Bed dressing can be just what the name suggests – giving your dowdy divan a splendid new set of

covers – or it can be making a bedhead, hanging up drapes or even building a four-poster frame,

which isn't nearly as daunting a project as it may seem. Use this book as a springboard for your own

ideas and mix projects together to produce a style that suits you.

BED LINEN

Above: Quilts are wonderfully cosy – whether 19th-century heirlooms, as here, or more modern pieces. Mix and match patterns for a country cottage look.

If your budget were unlimited, you could change your bed linen to suit your mood, the way we change our clothes. What a luxury to slide between luxurious silk sheets one night and crisp white cotton the next, followed by country florals, fleecy tartans, faded stripes and fresh, bright ginghams. However, practicality rules, and generally we dress our beds to match the room decor and stick with the same designs for years on end.

Layering many different prints and textures is a style of bed dressing that is popular at the moment, and it is both sophisticated and relaxed. The different fabrics can be combined successfully despite, or perhaps because of, their diversity. Frilled prairie prints can be teamed with cotton lace. Cosy tartans and faded patchworks create an attractive and comfortable style.

You can use bed linen to set a mood or create an atmosphere. If you want the room to look light and airy, the best choice is to go for white cotton sheets, pillow-cases and quilt covers. The whole look can be dressed up with hand-crocheted lace borders and cushion covers, mixing old and new together. You can add a gingham or floral bedcover or a patchwork quilt for a touch of country freshness, or a satin eiderdown for a Victorian look. A mixture of plain sheets, duvet cover and pillow-cases in different colours creates a modernist style that looks stunning with a black-framed bed. If you like the minimalist look, try a Japanese-style bed, with a textured, natural-coloured cover set off by black-tasselled cushions.

You can also choose from the huge array of imported textiles now on the market. Hot-coloured silks, batiks, ikats and hand-blocked prints can be layered and draped to re-create the atmosphere of another continent. Cover pillows with silk scarves and drape saris from a four-poster, then dye your sheets strong earthy yellows, red and browns for a rich layered look.

It is important to consider the feel of fabrics as well as the look. There is nothing to compare with the luxury of Egyptian cotton sheeting, especially after years of laundering, so never say no to hand-me-down pure cottons – even though they need ironing, unlike mixed polycotton sheets. Woollen blankets are wonderfully warm, but very itchy against the skin, so turn back a wide border of top sheet to cover the blanket. Velvet bed throws feel very luxurious and can be made from old velvet curtains. Edge and join panels with a rich braid for a medieval look.

Duvets have revolutionized bed making and children these days know nothing of "hospital corners" or the heaviness of a pile of blankets and bedspreads. There is no doubt that the duvet is an improvement in terms of comfort and an easy life, but duvets lack the style of sheets, blankets, bedspreads and eiderdowns. A good compromise is to dress up the bed with covers and cushions by day, then fold them back and shake out the duvet for a warm and comfortable night's rest.

Above: Duvets are warm and light, and dispense with having to make the bed. Home-made or bought duvet covers can be customized with details like these small ribbon ties.

Left: Nothing beats crisp white bed linen, and interesting edges and details make all the difference. Pure cotton will need ironing, but is worth the extra effort.

CUSHIONS

Above: A pile of cushions provides an instant face-lift to any bed. Here, a velvet-covered bolster is teamed with organza and cotton cushions and sari fabrics.

Cushions are the quickest and least expensive way of changing the mood and style of a room, so it is surprising that we don't all have cupboards bursting with alternative covers awaiting their chance to be the main feature in response to our prevailing mood. It is difficult to imagine having too many cushions because each one adds to the atmosphere of comfort and relaxation, which must be a priority in the bedroom.

The colour, texture, shape and size of cushions can all be used to add interest to a room. The same bedroom with a plain bed, carpet and neutral wall colour can be transformed by an arrangement of Chinese embroidered and tasselled satin cushions, rough homespun earthy-coloured bolsters or frilled red gingham squares mixed with patchworks and cotton lace. The mood each time will be entirely different. Other options to consider are Provencal prints, Indian hand-blocked cottons, rich brocades and satins, or tactile velvets. Bolsters can be used as the base for a luxurious pile of cushions. The secret is to use them to fill the angle between the mattress and the bedhead, then pile pillows and cushions on top to make a gentle slope at the perfect angle for a morning cup of tea or a book at bedtime. Wrap a bolster in a lace-edged tablecloth, tying up the ends with ribbon, Christmas-cracker-style, so that they spill out over the edge of the bed, or use velvet-edged ribbons, fancy cords and tassels for a flamboyant Renaissance look.

A comfortable cross between a bolster and loose cushions can be made by stitching a row of same-sized cushions together. Use cushions covered in the same fabric or choose a mixture of plain covers and co-ordinating prints. Sew one edge of each cushion together to make a single long, jointed cushion that is the same width as the bed.

Look out for fabric-remnant bins because they usually contain a wealth of short lengths that are ideal for cushion covers. It is also worth looking in haberdashery departments for dressmaker's trimmings like fringing, lace, braids, ribbons and beadwork borders. These are not as hardwearing as upholsterer's trimmings but cost a fraction of the price and are perfectly adequate for bedroom cushions.

Don't despair if you don't like sewing as covers can be made using iron-on hemming tape, strong double-sided carpet tape or pins, knots and ties. A cushion can be merely decorative and it is fun to dress up your bed during the day, particularly if it is going to be on show, then remove all the more fragile accessories at night. This sort of bed dressing is fun if you have the luxury of a guest room to decorate, because there will be periods when it stands empty but still needs to look welcoming.

If you have always thought that cushions just belonged in the living room and pillows were only for sleeping on, then perhaps it is time to consider giving cushions a bit of bed space too.

Above: Lace-edged cotton and organza create a wonderfully romantic look.

Left: Kilim-covered cushions make a fantastic display on a four-poster bed. Create the look at home by buying old pieces of fabric. Worn-out or threadbare sections can be discarded, leaving enough to cover the cushions.

DRAPES

A draped four-poster bed is like a room within a room – it is as warm, snug and dark as you wish it to be. Many stately homes and museums display ornately carved examples that would not be made now because of the time and expense involved. The beds of kings and queens were the grandest affairs, with intricately embroidered silk drapes. Although a comparable original would be prohibitively expensive, you can draw on the past for inspiration.

You can drape anything from chintz curtains to strings of beads, or perhaps floaty layers of net and muslin. You don't need a four-poster to have drapes, and there are all sorts of ways in which fabric can be gathered or hung to give a variety of different effects. A half-tester is a wooden box that is wall-mounted above the bed, with the fabric hung from the inside in two sections, to drape on either side of the bed. The effect can be solid and grand, or light and romantic, depending on the fabrics used. A simple semi-circular shelf can be fitted to the wall above the bed from which to drape a length of muslin, as described in the Draped Voile project. A staple gun is the ideal tool for this type of draping because it allows you to pleat the fabric as you attach it to the shelf. Another advantage is that it is very quick – you can drape a bed in this way in just an hour or two.

A mosquito net is a ready-made bed drape that simply needs a ceiling hook for installation. Evoke the African savannah by adding a few potted palms and fake animal-print rugs, or create an air of mystery with a deep colour on the walls to highlight the light drifts of net.

Drapes don't have to be delicate and lightweight but you do have to have a very sound structure to hold heavy fabrics. Sleeping under an over-stressed framework and metres of velvet or brocade will make you quite vulnerable. Beautiful satin brocades or embossed silks can often be found in the form of second-hand curtains and they can be used in combination with lighter voiles, organzas and muslins. Hang the heavy fabrics next to the wall with the lighter

Above: Lengths of muslin are suspended from the ceiling to cascade over the head and foot of the bed. Muslin is very inexpensive, so you can make the drapes as generous as you like. Any excess fabric can be left to spill across the floor.

ones on top to be draped over the bed. The richer fabric can be tied back with tasselled cords and bunched into shape to frame the wall around the bed.

If you have a bed with iron or wooden ends, you can hang a single length of fabric centrally and drape it casually over the bed ends. This is a very informal look but it still defines and visually encloses the sleeping area.

The most important thing to remember when draping a bed is that you will always need more fabric than you imagine. The success of the draped effect relies upon a generous amount of fabric to spill out on to the floor around the bed to add to the sense of luxurious splendour!

Above: Extravagant drapes of striped fabric complement the ornate carvings on the four-poster bed. The same fabric is repeated at the windows, creating an opulent, co-ordinated look.

Left: This ingenious treatment involves suspending generous drapes of muslin from tasselled cords hanging from the ceiling. As muslin is very lightweight, you will not have to worry about heavy-duty fixings for the cord.

BEDHEADS

Above: A turned-pine headboard was customized with a distressed paint finish and a stamped pattern, while the poles were painted in a contrasting colour. The stars were stamped on to the wood with a cut kitchen sponge dipped into emulsion.

Beds without headboards create a very utilitarian and temporary impression. A headboard can make the simplest of beds into an item of furniture with definite style, and the possibilities really are endless.

Existing headboards can be re-vamped and given a totally different character using paint, rope, upholstery, drapes or fabric wraps. An old padded headboard, for instance, may be very comfortable but quite unpleasant to look at. All you need is a length of fabric and a staple gun to give it a completely new appearance. A leopard-skin-printed velvet; a rich chocolate brocaded satin; a woven Mexican striped blanket or a black and white hounds-tooth check all have strong designs to give instant attitude to a dingy but comfortable padded headboard.

You may prefer something a little more subtle. A new turned-pine bedhead can be rubbed down with sandpaper, then painted with two coats of matt paint. The first should be a bright colour and the second a lot darker. When the paint has dried, rub it back with fine-grade sandpaper or wire wool to reveal flashes of the brighter colour beneath. Paint initials or marriage dates along the top rail to transform a mass-produced bed into a family heirloom.

Some iron beds have ornate detailing which deserves to be seen, while the more utilitarian styles can look rather severe. Both types need a good supply of pillows, cushions and bolsters to make them comfortable. A plain iron bed can be made to look soft and welcoming with layers of frilly bed linen and a soft padding of eiderdowns and pillows.

If your bed is to be pushed up against a wall or wedged into a corner, you can stand a bedhead behind it without actually fixing it to the bed. This means that you can use virtually anything at all – a length of picket fence, a papier-mâché construction, an inflated lilo, wooden pallets or woven foam strips, to name just a few of the more unusual possibilities.

Above: A woven willow headboard becomes a feature in this rustic bedroom. Be creative when looking for bedheads – rural garden shops often have lengths of interesting fencing which can be used in the bedroom.

Right: This beautiful distressed-effect bedhead is complemented by the pile of lace cushions, creating a country look in the bedroom. For a distressed paint effect, choose two colours, one darker than the other. Paint the darker coat first, and leave to dry. Apply the second coat, and, before it has completely dried, rub it back slightly with a cloth so that the darker colour shows through.

ALTERNATIVE BEDS

Above: Sleigh beds create a period atmosphere, and can occasionally be found at a reasonable price.

If you would like to recreate a period feel, have a difficult space to fill, or are simply looking for a more unusual effect, take a look at some of these "alternative" approaches to the traditional bed with headboard.

Futons are unstructured cotton-filled mattresses from Japan. They are designed to be rolled up during the day to provide more living space and to air the mattress. Although they are designed to lie on the floor, they can be used on upholstered bed bases or on slatted wooden bases. Futons feel very hard when you first sleep on them but with perseverance you will find them to be among the most comfortable and restful mattresses to sleep on.

In Scandinavia and Brittany, there is a tradition of building beds into alcoves. Wooden shutter doors close them off like cupboards. This does make a room smaller, but all signs of the bed disappear and the room can then have an alternative daytime personality. This sort of bed is really cosy as it is enclosed on three sides. Pile the space with bolsters, pillows and quilts for extra comfort. A cupboard bed is perfect for a draughty cottage or as a novelty bed for a child, as it provides a feeling of security.

Sometimes it is good to put your feet up and have a rest without actually taking to your bed during the day. A chaise is halfway between a bed and a sofa, and perfect for an afternoon nap. Chaises were popular during the Victorian era, and many sprung and upholstered chaises can still be found today. A good warm throw such as a crazy quilt or a hand-knitted Afghan is all you need to complete your daybed.

A hammock makes a most relaxing daybed because it instils a sensation of total idleness. All you need is a couple of strong wall fixtures situated the right distance apart and a hammock to string between them. A real advantage is that you can remove and store a hammock when it is not in use. Increase the comfort level with lots of cushions and a soft quilt, then settle back with a good book and some mood music.

Above: This iron bed is given the daybed treatment. The cushions are piled to make it suitable for sitting and lounging during the day, while the bed can easily be used by guests at night.

Right: This bed takes its cue from the cupboard beds that are such a feature of Scandinavian interiors. Drawers below the bed provide useful room for storage in a small space.

BEACH-MAT BED

A simple four-poster frame can be built to fit around an existing base and mattress. This requires only basic carpentry skills as the timber can be cut to size when you buy it, and just needs drilling and screwing together. The wood used here is basic construction timber that has been left in its natural state, but you could colour it with woodstain or paint.

Grass beach mats are perfect for hanging around the four-poster, especially if your room is decorated with natural fabrics and colours. The loosely stitched grass strips allow a soft golden light to filter through.

YOU WILL NEED

♦ grass beach mats
♦ packet of brass paper fasteners
♦ rough twine
♦ scissors
♦ odd-shaped shells, pebbles and driftwood

1 Fold one short edge of each beach mat over the top rail of the four-poster frame. Push paper fasteners through the mats just below the rail and open out the prongs. Use four fasteners along the top of each beach mat.

2 The mats are edged with different coloured tape that makes fine stripes around the bed. Arrange the mats to make the most of this striping.

3 Decide how many blinds you want to tie up – maybe all, or just a select few. You will need about 1m/1yd of rough twine for each mat to be rolled up. Cut the lengths required and tie some shells, pebbles and bits of driftwood randomly along the length and at each end of the twine.

4 Dangle over the top rail and use them to tie back the rolled-up blinds.

RENAISSANCE HEADBOARD

In this bedroom, dramatic effects have been used to create a very distinctive atmosphere, with the scale of the painting dominating the room. It's a good idea to visit a museum shop for the best range and quality of art posters – you are certain to find something for all tastes. You can apply a crackle glaze or antiquing varnish to the poster if you wish to add an authentically aged Renaissance look.

To complete the look, the warmth of velvet is juxtaposed with the cool crispness of crocheted lace and cotton – both are luxurious when set against the marble-effect walls.

YOU WILL NEED

- wallpaper paste
- poster
- MDF (width of poster x height of poster plus mattress to floor measurement), plus allowance for frame
- paste brush
- pencil
- ruler
- picture rail moulding (height of poster x 2, plus width x 1)
- mitring block
- small saw
- viridian green emulsion paint
- paintbrushes
- gold spray paint
- fine-grade sandpaper
- glue gun and glue sticks
- crackle-glaze varnish
- red artist's oil colour
- clean cloths
- clear varnish
- drill and fixtures to attach MDF to bed frame (depending on the type of bed)

1 Mix wallpaper paste according to the manufacturer's instructions. Mark the position of the poster on the MDF and apply paste to that section.

2 Smooth the poster on to the board and leave to dry. Any air bubbles should disappear as the glue dries.

3 Measure and mark the lengths of picture rail moulding needed for the poster frame. The frame goes along the top of the poster and down both sides to mattress height. Saw the corners on a mitring block.

5 Protect your work surface, then spray a coat of gold spray paint over the green. Leave to dry.

7 Paint the whole surface of the poster with crackle-glaze varnish, following the manufacturer's instructions. Leave the varnish to crackle.

4 Paint the frame with an undercoat of viridian green emulsion paint. Leave to dry.

6 Rub the frame with fine-grade sandpaper, so that the gold is lifted on the highest ridges to reveal the green beneath. Do not overdo the sanding. Use a glue gun to stick the picture frame around the edges of the poster.

8 Use a cloth to rub artist's oil colour into the surface. Red is used here but any strong or dark colour will also work well. Rub the oil paint right into the cracks and cover the whole surface area.

9 Use a clean, soft cloth to rub the oil paint off the surface. The colour will stay in the cracks to form the crackle-glazed effect. Apply several coats of clear varnish to the poster. When dry, attach the headboard to the bed frame, using the drill and fixtures.

CANOPIED BED

A simple draped canopy is a great way to define a sleeping area without completely enclosing it. The muslin is draped over a wooden plant support. The natural character of the twigs combines very well with the unbleached muslin. Muslin is inexpensive, so buy more than you need – any extra will make a pretty cascade at the end of the bed.

YOU WILL NEED

- at least 12m/13yd unbleached muslin
- iron-on hemming tape
- iron
- rustic plant support
- rubber bands
- twine
- scissors
- ceiling hook

1 Turn up a hem at each end of the fabric and use iron-on hemming tape to make a neat seam. Find the middle of the fabric length and bunch and wrap the muslin around the narrow end of the plant support at this point.

2 Pull the fabric into a pleasing shape, then secure it in this position with rubber bands.

3 Wind the twine around the rubber bands, to cover them. Wrap the twine decoratively around the fabric, then tie off the ends.

4 Attach a ceiling hook centrally above the bed. Hang the plant support from it, using extra twine if necessary. Drape the muslin either side of the support and over the bed ends. Allow any excess to spill around the bed.

VICTORIAN LACE

Nothing looks more romantic than a brass bed covered with lace-trimmed white bed linen. Make layers of scallops and frills on sheets, bolsters, pillows and bedcovers. Start by buying a good cotton duvet cover with a scalloped edge. Trawl second-hand shops and flea markets for lace-edged tablecloths, dressing table runners, tray cloths and curtain panels. Look out for old white cotton sheets with embroidered edges to add interest.

YOU WILL NEED
◆ plain white bed linen
◆ selection of lacy tablecloths, tray cloths, mats, chair backs or dressing table runners
◆ pins
◆ iron-on hemming tape or needle and white thread
◆ bolsters
◆ rubber bands
◆ white ribbon or raffia

1 Select suitably sized lace additions to make central panels or corner details on the pillow-cases and duvet cover. Pin them in position.

2 Use iron-on hemming tape and an iron to bond the two layers together, or slip-stitch them in place.

3 Roll the bolster up in a lace-edged tablecloth and bunch up the ends, securing them with rubber bands.

4 Tie bows of ribbon or raffia over the gathered ends and let the lace edging drape over the edge of the bed.

CHILD'S BEDROOM

Small children like the security of enclosed

sleeping spaces and older children relish

the privacy, especially if their room is

shared with a brother or sister. In this

project, MDF panels are positioned

around an existing bed. They can be

attached to the bed base or simply rested

in a corner so that they enclose the space

but cannot be pushed over.

The animal stencils used to decorate the

MDF panels and the bed linen can also

be used on the walls.

YOU WILL NEED

- ◆ 2 sheets MDF, 122cm/48in x width of the bed
- ◆ 1 sheet MDF, 122cm/48in x length of the bed, plus 5cm/2in
- ◆ 5 x 2.5cm/2 x 1in baton, 122cm/48in long
- ◆ drill, with size 10 bit
- ◆ screwdriver and suitable screw fixings
- ◆ pale grey emulsion paint
- ◆ paintbrush
- ◆ paper
- ◆ spray adhesive
- ◆ stencil card
- ◆ scalpel or craft knife
- ◆ cutting mat or thick card
- ◆ white pillow-case
- ◆ iron
- ◆ masking tape
- ◆ fabric paints in red, blue and yellow
- ◆ plate
- ◆ stencil brushes
- ◆ white sheet or duvet cover
- ◆ soft and hard pencils
- ◆ jigsaw
- ◆ fine-grade sandpaper
- ◆ stencil paints (optional)

1 The shorter pieces of MDF are used for the head and foot of the bed. To make the bed surround, screw the baton to butt up to one 122cm/48in edge of the head and foot pieces. Butt the long piece of MDF up against the baton on the bedhead, at right angles, and screw in place. Repeat with the foot, to make a three-sided surround for the bed. The bed surround will now be reasonably stable, but it is advisable to position the long side against a wall. Paint the surround with pale grey emulsion.

2 To stencil the bed linen, enlarge the templates from the back of the book on to paper. Spray the backs lightly with spray adhesive and stick them on to sheets of stencil card.

3 Cut out the stencils carefully, using a scalpel or craft knife on a cutting mat or sheet of thick card to protect your work surface.

5 Wash and iron the fabric to be stencilled. Place some paper inside the pillow-case. Position the first stencil, holding it in place with masking tape.

7 Position the next stencil, being very careful not to smudge the first one, and then stencil the second animal in another colour.

4 Peel off the paper patterns to leave the cut-out stencils.

6 Spread each of the fabric paints on to the plate. Using a stencil brush, dab the first colour on to the pillow-case. Apply the paint sparingly as the colour is best when built up gradually.

8 Position a third stencil and apply the final colour. Continue alternating the stencils and colours to complete the pillow-case. Decorate the sheet or duvet cover in the same way.

9 To make the "window", enlarge the crocodile template in sections so that you end up with a good window-size pattern. Then tape the different sections together.

11 Place the pattern face-up on the MDF and transfer by drawing over the outline with a hard pencil. Drill a hole at any point on the outline as the insertion point for the jigsaw blade.

13 Rub down all the edges of the cut-out crocodile shape using fine-grade sandpaper.

10 Rub the back of the pattern outline with a soft pencil.

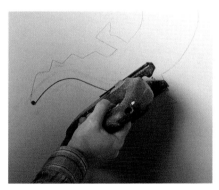

12 Use the jigsaw to cut out the crocodile shape. Work slowly and hold the blade vertically so that it cuts at its own speed without being pushed or dragged into the MDF.

14 Stencil a frieze of animals around the inside of the bed screen to co-ordinate with the bed linen. You can use the fabric paints for this, or matching stencil paints.

GINGHAM HEADBOARD

This headboard conversion creates a fresh new style with added comfort. The gingham is backed with quilter's wadding. The headboard should be rectangular in shape and can be solid or of a slatted or spindled type. Measure the width and height of the headboard, then double the height measurement so that the gingham folds in half over the top.

YOU WILL NEED

- iron-on quilter's wadding
- dressmaker's scissors
- iron
- gingham, width of the headboard x twice the height, plus seam allowance on all edges
- iron-on hemming tape
- needle and matching sewing thread
- 2m/2yd red ribbon
- pins
- tape measure

1 Cut the wadding to the size of the headboard. Press one end of the gingham on to the wadding. The other end of the gingham will fold over the headboard back. Leave a large seam allowance all around the edge.

2 Fold the seams over and tuck the corners in neatly. Use iron-on hemming tape or a needle and thread to secure the edges. As the hems will be on the inside of the cover, they will not be visible.

3 To make the ties, cut the ribbon into 16 equal lengths.

4 Pin, then sew four ribbons along the inside edges of each side of the gingham cover. Use a tape measure to ensure the ribbons at the front and back are equally spaced. Fold the cover over the headboard and tie the ribbons in bows to finish.

JAPANESE FUTON

This stylish bedroom exudes a typically Japanese sense of order and calm. Wooden pallets were used for the bed base. These come in different sizes, but they can be sawn down and stacked to make a bed of the right size. The beautiful cream cotton bedcover is a decorator's dustsheet. Such dustsheets are incredibly cheap, so you can have the minimalist look for a minimal outlay.

YOU WILL NEED

- ◆ wooden pallets
- ◆ medium- and fine-grade sandpaper
- ◆ light-coloured woodstain
- ◆ paintbrush
- ◆ 2m/2yd black cotton cord
- ◆ scissors
- ◆ needle and thread
- ◆ decorator's dustsheet
- ◆ 2 black tassels
- ◆ square cream-coloured cushion

1 Rub down the wooden pallets using first medium-grade, then fine-grade sandpaper.

2 Apply a coat of woodstain to seal and colour the wood. Lay the pallets on the floor to make a bed base.

3 Cut six 30cm/12in lengths of black cord. Make each length into a loop tied with a reef knot.

4 Slip-stitch the knotted cords on to the dustsheet to make three rows of two cords down the centre of the bed. Spread the dustsheet on the bed and fold it neatly over the pillows. Sew two black tassels on to the cushion and place it on the pillows. Tuck the dustsheet under the mattress all the way around the bed.

INDIAN TEMPLE BEDHEAD

Indian temple wall paintings are the inspiration for this arch-shaped bedhead. The bedroom feels as if it has been magically transported thousands of miles, but the real magic here comes in a simple pot of paint. Before painting the bedhead, set the mood with a deep rust-coloured wash on the walls. If you can, use a water-based distemper for an authentic powdery bloom. If you are using emulsion, thin it with water and use random brush strokes for a patchy, mottled look.

The arch is chalked into the wall using a paper template. Once the pattern has been chalked up, the painting is a real pleasure.

. YOU WILL NEED

- ◆ large roll of brown parcel wrap
- ◆ felt-tipped pen
- ◆ masking tape (optional)
- ◆ scissors
- ◆ spray adhesive
- ◆ chalk
- ◆ water-based paint in dark blue, bright blue and red
- ◆ plate
- ◆ kitchen sponge
- ◆ sandy cream emulsion paint
- ◆ medium and fine paintbrushes
- ◆ fine-grade sandpaper

1 Refer to the diagram on page 38. Transfer a half-arch on to brown parcel wrap, enlarging it as required using a grid system. Alternatively, tape a sheet of brown parcel wrap on the wall and draw the half-arch directly on to it, following the pattern shape.

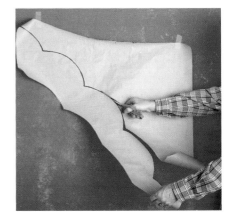

2 Cut out the half-arch shape using a pair of scissors.

3 Position the paper pattern on the wall with spray adhesive and draw around the edges with chalk.

4 Flip the pattern and draw around it to produce the second half of the arch.

5 Spread some dark blue paint on to a plate and use a damp sponge to dab it on to the central panel. Don't cover the background completely but leave some of the wall colour showing through. When the paint is dry, apply the bright blue paint over the dark blue in the same way.

6 When the paint is dry, paint the arch in sandy cream emulsion, using a medium-size paintbrush.

7 When the sandy cream paint is dry, rub it back in places with fine-grade sandpaper, to give a faded effect.

8 Outline the inside and outside of the arch with the red paint, using a fine paintbrush. Support your painting hand with your free hand and use the width of the brush to make a single line.

9 Outline the outer red stripe with a thinner dark blue line. Work as described in the previous step, keeping the line as clean as possible.

10 Leave to dry, then use fine-grade sandpaper to soften any hard edges and give the arch the naturally faded appearance of an old temple wall.

ROMANTIC NETTING

Even if you have no practical need for mosquito netting, the light and airy beauty of this project makes it ideal for the bedrooms of urban romantics who dream of being in the Punjab or on the Serengeti plains. Netting like this can be bought from camping shops and comes complete with the spoked wooden coronet that opens like a fan. The spokes are then decorated with dangling glass ornaments to make the netting look more exotic than utilitarian. The netting can also be dyed in any pale colour.

YOU WILL NEED
- mosquito netting, with coronet and fixings
- dangling glass ornaments and earrings
- fine wire
- long-nosed pliers
- ceiling hook

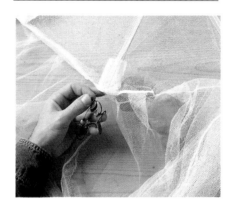

1 Fan out the spokes of the wooden coronet and fit them into the channels of the netting.

2 Thread assorted ornaments and earrings on to lengths of fine wire to make decorative pendants.

3 Thread the wire ends through the netting at the bottom of the spokes. Use long-nosed pliers to twist the ends together to secure them.

4 Attach the ring and rope provided to the centre of the coronet. Hang the net from a ceiling hook above the bed.

40

BLACK AND WHITE PRINTS

nImagine being able to decorate soft furnishings with any image of your choice. There is now a special transparent gel available which enables you to transfer black and white or colour images on to fabric. The image can then be sealed to make it resistant to wear and tear. By enlarging or reducing the images on a photocopier, you can obtain a selection of prints that will fit perfectly on to the item you wish to decorate.

You can use the same process to monogram your bed linen, but as the image will be reversed once transferred, you will have to photocopy any lettering on to acetate first.

YOU WILL NEED

- ◆ photocopies of chosen images
- ◆ scissors
- ◆ plain-coloured cotton cushion cover
- ◆ iron
- ◆ plastic carrier bag
- ◆ image-transfer gel
- ◆ paintbrush
- ◆ soft cloth
- ◆ sheet of acetate (optional)

2 Cut away all the excess paper, leaving only the images that you want to transfer.

1 Choose your images and make the required number of copies. Here, several copies of the same image have been made to form a frame around the central portrait.

3 To design the cushion cover, arrange the images on a flat surface. Experiment with spacing until you are happy with the design.

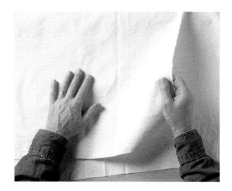

4 Pre-wash and iron the cushion cover. This is important because glazes used to stiffen fabrics may affect the transfer process. Place the cover on a plastic carrier bag to protect your work surface.

5 Paint a thick layer of transfer gel on to the first photocopy, being sure to cover it completely.

6 Place the image face-down on the cushion cover and rub the back with a soft cloth.

7 Repeat steps 5 and 6 with all the images, ensuring that they are positioned accurately before you make contact with the fabric. Leave to transfer overnight.

8 Soak the cloth with clean water and use it to saturate the photocopy paper.

9 Keep the cloth wet and begin to rub away the paper, working from the centre outwards. The images will have transferred on to the fabric. When all the paper has been removed, leave the fabric to dry.

10 Apply a final fixing coat of the transfer gel to the prints and leave to dry completely.

12 Transfer the initials as described in steps 5 to 10. The transfer process will reverse the initials once more, so that they are now the right way round.

11 You can use the same process to monogram your bed linen. Photocopy the initials on to a sheet of acetate. Then turn the acetate over and photocopy from the acetate on to paper to reverse. Cut out the print.

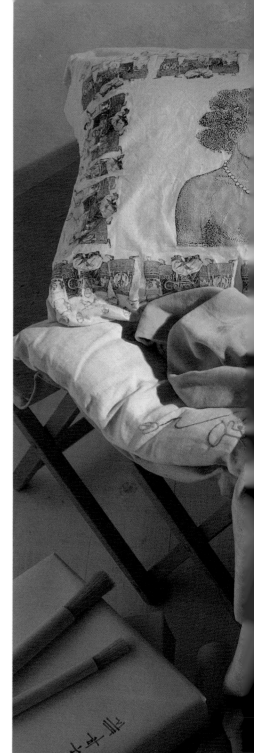

THE AMERICAN DREAM

Lie in state every night, draped in the Stars and Stripes. The timber-clad walls and peg-rail above the bed give the room a ranch-house feel that looks great alongside the flags.

You could, of course, use the flag of your choice, although some may be more difficult to obtain than others.

YOU WILL NEED

- ◆ 2 large flags
- ◆ pillow
- ◆ packet of safety pins
- ◆ needle and thread
- ◆ wooden buttons
- ◆ quilt

1 Fold one of the flags around the pillow and use safety pins to close the long seam.

2 Sew three wooden buttons along one pillow edge to hold the seam closed. Leave the other edge open so the pillow can be removed.

3 Select an assortment of wooden buttons to attach around the edge and across the centre of the second flag.

4 Lay the flag over the quilt. Sew on the buttons, stitching through both the flag and the quilt, so that the layers are held together.

ANIMAL CUSHIONS

Animal prints have never been more popular and the quality of fake fur now available is fantastic. The distinctive boldness of the cowhide print chosen here makes great cushion covers. The low bed is draped with lengths of silky smooth velvet tiger- and leopard-skin fabric that spill on to the floor, adding to the languorous atmosphere. This project doesn't have to be permanent – so bring out the bedding for wild weekends.

YOU WILL NEED

♦ card
♦ scissors
♦ button blanks
♦ small pieces of black velvet
♦ hemmed squares of cowhide print, 5cm/2in smaller than the cushions
♦ black velvet cushions
♦ needle and thread
♦ tiger- and leopard-skin fabrics

1 Cut a circle of card approximately 1cm/½in larger all round than the button blanks. Use the card pattern to cut circles of black velvet.

2 Cover the top of each button blank with a velvet circle, tucking in the edges so that they catch on to the spikes underneath.

3 Press the backing in place to make neatly covered black velvet buttons.

4 Position a hemmed cowhide fabric square diagonally on each cushion and stitch in place. Sew a black button on to the centre, stitching through both the cowhide print and the black velvet cushion. Arrange the tiger- and leopard-skin fabrics over the bed.

HALF-TESTER

This positively regal half-tester draped with cool white cotton will add majestic splendour to your bedroom. This sort of bed was most popular around the second half of the 19th century, when draped four-posters became less fashionable. The style imitates the ornate four-poster but is actually a box made to fit against the wall and extend no more than a third of the length of the bed,

often much less. This half-tester is made out of a batten and picture frame moulding and adorned with plaster scrolls bought from a DIY store.

The wall plaque is not strictly a part of the half-tester but it fits in perfectly, looking down from between the drapes.

Use a fine white fabric such as voile, muslin or cotton sheeting for the drapes.

YOU WILL NEED
- plastercast head wall hanging
- backing paper
- shellac
- paintbrushes
- gold spray paint
- black emulsion or poster paint
- cloth
- wire wool
- 2 scrolled plaster decorations
- larger scrolled plaster decoration
- 155cm/62in fancy picture frame moulding
- woodstain (optional)
- 5 x 2.5cm/2 x 1in batten, 115cm/46in long
- 155cm/62in doorframe moulding
- saw
- mitring block
- glue gun and glue sticks
- 1cm/½in wooden dowelling, 10cm/4in long
- curtain rings with clips
- heavy-duty staple gun or eyelet screws
- at least 10m/11yd fine white fabric
- scissors
- drill, with appropriate drill bit
- wall plugs
- screwdriver and long screws

1 Place the plastercast head on a piece of backing paper to protect your work surface. Apply a coat of shellac to seal the surface.

2 Allow the first coat to dry (for about 20 minutes), then apply a second coat of shellac. Allow to dry.

3 Spray the head with gold spray paint. Allow to dry. Paint over the gold with black emulsion or poster paint. Cover the gold completely.

4 Before the paint dries, rub most of it off using a slightly damp cloth. The black will have dulled the brassiness of the gold beneath.

5 Burnish the high spots such as the cheek bones, nose and brows using wire wool. Give the scrolled decorations and picture frame moulding the same treatment, or stain them with your chosen colour of woodstain. Cut the batten into one 75cm/30in and one 40cm/16in length. Cut the doorframe and picture frame moulding into one 75cm/30in and two 40cm/16in lengths.

6 Using a mitring block, saw the corners on the picture frame and doorframe moulding that are to meet to make up the box shape. These will be both ends of the longest pieces and one end of each of the shorter ones.

7 Glue the mitred door mouldings at the edges and fit the box shape together, placing the longest batten at the back. Surround the front three sides with the fancy moulding. Then glue the short batten in the centre of the piece as a reinforcement.

8 Cut the dowelling into two 5cm/ 2in lengths and glue one piece into each top corner of the half-tester at the back of the moulding. They will act as supports for the scroll decorations.

9 Apply hot glue to each length of dowelling and then stick the corner scrolls in place.

10 Fix the curtain rings with clips at equal distances around the inside of the mouldings, using a heavy-duty staple gun or eyelet screws.

11 Cut the fabric in half along its length. Before putting up the half-tester, clip one length of fabric around one side to see how much fabric falls between each pair of clips. It will be easier to hang the drapes once the half-tester is in place if you have worked out the spacing in advance. Remove the fabric. Fix the half-tester to the wall near the ceiling, using appropriate fixings, and fix the plaster head to the wall. Clip the drapes in place and drape the fabric around the bed, so that it spills out on to the floor.

Left: The decorative moulding and plaster scrolls create a sumptuous antique effect at little expense.

DRAPED VOILE

A simple semi-circular shelf is fixed on the wall to provide a long drop for this pretty length of voile. The voile is pleated directly on to the shelf and stapled in place, then allowed to fall back over the staples to make a soft valance effect.

YOU WILL NEED

- ◆ tape measure
- ◆ cotton voile (see step 1)
- ◆ semi-circular wooden shelf
- ◆ dark plum emulsion paint
- ◆ paintbrush
- ◆ drill, with appropriate drill bit
- ◆ wall plugs
- ◆ screwdriver and shelf fixtures
- ◆ scissors
- ◆ iron-on hemming tape
- ◆ iron
- ◆ staple gun and staples

1 Measure the width of your bed and from the ceiling to the floor. The cotton voile should be a little larger than this to allow for the fold at the top and extra drapery on the floor. Paint the wooden shelf with emulsion. When dry, fix the shelf to the wall, about 30cm/12in below the ceiling.

2 Cut the fabric in half lengthwise. With iron-on hemming tape, make seams along the cut edges. Staple one end of each length to the underside of the shelf, pleating each side as you go.

3 At the top of one drape, lift about 50cm/20in on to the shelf and staple along the edge to secure it. Staple the second length in the same way. Allow the voile to fall back down to create the soft valancing effect, and arrange the drapes around the bedhead and on the floor.

SPACE BED

At last, a terrestrial bed with all the glamour and sparkle of space travel. If the very thought of a night in has you reaching for your sci-fi videos, why not relax wrapped in your very own shimmering silver space-blanket bed?

The shape of this headboard is reminiscent of a 1950s tailfin, but you can choose almost any bold shape that can be cut out of MDF with a jigsaw. You can buy space blankets from outdoor pursuits stores that sell camping equipment. A thin, smooth blanket is used for the cover and a thicker-textured one for the buttoning.

YOU WILL NEED

- 1 sheet MDF, width of the bed x height to bed base, plus approximately 1m/1yd
- pen
- ruler
- string
- drawing pin
- jigsaw
- fine-grade sandpaper
- polyester duvet
- staple gun and staples
- thin silver insulating material (the type used by athletes)
- broad, woven adhesive tape
- tape measure
- thicker-textured silver insulating material (the type used under camping mattresses)
- scissors

1 Draw a line across the width of the MDF about 40cm/16in down from the top edge. Tie a 40cm/16in length of string to a drawing pin and tie a pen to the other end. Push the pin into the line, just in from the left edge of the board. Pull the string taut and adjust its length to reach the top lefthand corner of the board. Using the string as the arm of a pair of compasses, draw a curve from the top of the board down to the line.

2 Cut out the shape around the curve and along the line with a jigsaw. Sand down the edges.

4 Staple the edges to the MDF, folding them under and tucking them in to get as even a finish as possible.

6 Stick a strip of broad woven tape over the edges of the silver material to cover the staples and give a neat finish.

3 Fold the duvet around the MDF to give a smooth covering across the front. Fold the edges to the back.

5 Lay the covered shape on to the thin silver insulating material. Fold the edges to the back and staple.

7 Turn the bedhead over and adjust any wrinkles in the "space blanket".

8 Mark points at intervals of 24cm/9½in along a piece of string.

9 Use the piece of string to measure the positions of the quilting buttons on the covered headboard. Mark each point with a small square of woven tape.

10 Cut strips of the thicker-textured insulating material into squares to use as "buttons" for the quilting.

11 Staple a silver button on top of each tape square. Make sure that the silver covers up the tape. The tape strengthens the thin silver material and prevents the staples from tearing it.

12 Push down hard with the staple gun, so that the staple penetrates right through to the MDF. Continue stapling the buttons in place until the whole headboard is quilted.

Above: The quilted effect is achieved simply by stapling through the top material to the duvet lining.

STICK HEADBOARD

Dress up the wall behind a simple bed with an unusual trellis made from woven twigs and branches. The trellis is very lightweight and is easily fixed in place. Continue the theme with twig accessories ranging from chairs to cache-pots, and complement the decor with crisply starched white sheets and pretty cushion covers. Country garden centres are always worth a visit, because trellis-work like this is handmade and producers often use local garden centres as outlets.

YOU WILL NEED
- garden raffia
- scissors
- handmade twig trellis
- masonry nails or cavity wall fixtures
- hammer

1 Divide the raffia into two bunches of about twelve strands each. Knot one end of each bunch.

2 Plait the strands to make two braids about 10cm/4in long.

3 Tie the two plaits on to the trellis about 25cm/10in from each end.

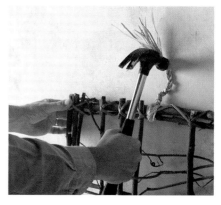

4 Use masonry nails or cavity wall fixtures to attach the plaits to the wall above the bed, suspending the trellis behind the bed.

CORRUGATED HEADBOARD

Corrugated cardboard has been liberated from its useful role as a packaging material as designers realize its potential and versatility. It is strong, rigid, insulating, economical and light as a feather. This project celebrates the natural cardboard colour, but coloured sheets are also available and are great for adding decorative touches.

Corrugated cardboard is perfect for experimentation. It can be glued into layers to make a thicker material that is still lightweight and easy to cut through. If you make a mistake, the material is so inexpensive you can always start again!

YOU WILL NEED
- glue gun and glue sticks
- 5 x 2.5cm/2 x 1in batten, to fit around the edges of the MDF
- rectangle of MDF, to fit behind the bed
- roll of corrugated cardboard 1m/1yd high
- set square
- scissors
- staple gun and staples
- ruler
- pencil
- scalpel or craft knife
- cutting mat or thick card
- small rubber roller

2 Place a large piece of corrugated cardboard over the front of the MDF. Use a set square to press against and crease the cardboard neatly for folding at the corners.

1 Use the glue gun to stick the thin strips of wood to the back of the MDF around the edges. This will all be hidden by the corrugated cardboard, so any glue drips will not show.

3 Fold the cardboard neatly around the corners in the same way that you would wrap a parcel.

4 Trim away any excess cardboard that would cause the folded corners to look bulky.

6 Carefully staple the cardboard along the strips of wood, keeping it taut as you go along.

8 Use the rubber roller to flatten down the ridges.

5 Staple the flaps down, pressing the staple gun firmly against the cardboard from above to prevent any kickback that may cause the staples to protrude.

7 Cut four strips of cardboard 7.5cm/3in wide, and approximately 45cm/18in long.

9 Fold the strips into three along their length, so that they are 2.5cm/1in wide. Again, use the rubber roller to flatten the strips.

10 Position the strips to form a diamond shape in the centre of the headboard. Allow the ends to overlap each other. Staple the strips in place.

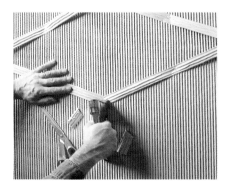

11 Cut through the two overlapping layers with scissors to mitre the corners. Staple the strips as closely as possible to the mitred ends.

12 For the spiral turrets, cut seven 50cm/20in strips of cardboard. One long edge of each strip is cut at an angle: Cut the first two strips along a line sloping from one short edge of 10cm/4in to the other short edge of 5cm/2in. Cut the second two strips from one edge of 12cm/4¾in to the other of 5cm/2in. Cut the next two from 14cm/5½in to 5cm/2in. Cut the last strip from 16cm/6¼in to 5cm/2in.

13 Starting at the widest end, roll up the cardboard with the ridges on the outside. Keep the base straight.

14 Use the glue gun to stick down the end of each turret.

15 Arrange the turrets on top of the headboard so that the tallest one is in the middle. Stick them down using the hot glue gun. Use plenty of glue in the middle and less towards the outside to achieve a good bond without any mess.

LOVE PILLOWS

Make sure the message gets across by stencilling the word "love" on your pillows in both English and French. The typeface used is the graphic designer's favourite, Gill (bold), chosen for its stylish simplicity. The word has been enlarged on a photocopier to 18cm/7in long. Always wash and iron the fabric before stencilling to rid it of any glazes that could block the colour absorption.

YOU WILL NEED

- ◆ photocopied enlargement of the words
- ◆ spray adhesive
- ◆ 2 pieces of stencil card
- ◆ scalpel or craft knife
- ◆ cutting mat or thick card
- ◆ sheet of thin card
- ◆ white cotton pillow-cases
- ◆ red fabric paint
- ◆ plate
- ◆ stencil brush
- ◆ iron

1 Enlarge the templates to the required size. Spray the backs of the photocopies with spray adhesive and stick them on to the stencil card.

2 Cut out the letters with a scalpel or craft knife on a cutting mat. The O, A and R need ties to retain the internal letter features, so draw them in "bridges" before you cut out the letters with the scalpel.

3 Place a sheet of thin card inside the pillow-case, so that the colour does not bleed through to the other side.

4 Spread some fabric paint on to a plate and use a stencil brush to stencil the letters. Be sparing with the paint. You can always build up the colour if necessary, but too much paint will cause problems. Leave the paint to dry. Follow the manufacturer's instructions to seal the stencilling with a hot iron.

CHINTZ HEADBOARD

Give your padded headboard a face-lift using old chintz curtains. The fabric improves with age as the colours fade and mellow, and it looks wonderful teamed with crisp white cotton, handmade quilts or plaid woollen blankets.

Use the very best section of pattern for the bedhead and tuck remaining lengths under the mattress to form a valance. If you prefer a more permanent valance, you could sew pleated lengths of the same chintz fabric around the edges of a fitted sheet.

YOU WILL NEED

♦ pair of floral chintz curtains

♦ scissors

♦ tape measure

♦ headboard

♦ pencil

♦ staple gun and staples

1 Trim the curtains to get rid of any thick seams, curtain tape and bulky hems. Cut a strip of curtain long enough to fold over the front and on to the back of the headboard at the sides, top and bottom. Smooth it over the front of the headboard then move to the back. Draw any curved corners on to the back of the fabric.

2 Cut notches in the fabric right up to the drawn line, so that the fabric will fit the curve without puckering. Staple each cut strip on to the headboard.

3 Pull down the top flap tautly and staple it on to the headboard.

4 Pull up the bottom flap tautly and staple it in place. Staple both side edges in the same way. Cut a panel of fabric to cover all the stapled edges on the back. Turn in the edges and staple the panel flat on to the backing board, so that no top or side edges are visible.

CUSHIONS

Dress up a pile of plain cushions and transform the atmosphere of your bedroom in an afternoon. The embellishments used here are dressmaker's trimmings which are available in a wide range of materials, shapes, colours and sizes. Upholstery and soft-furnishing trimmings tend to be more expensive and the range is limited, so it is well worth looking out for a dressmaking specialist. Market stallholders often carry haberdashery offcuts, with short lengths of fringing, beading, braids and lace which are ideal for embellishing cushions. Tie tassels and cord around the ends of a bolster cushion, for example, or embellish a plain black cushion with an unusual motif.

YOU WILL NEED
- 3 cushions: 2 velvet and 1 silk
- fringing
- needle and matching threads
- pencil
- pair of compasses
- thin card
- scissors
- pins
- black lace and fringing
- black bobble trimmings
- tape measure
- silver insulating material
- cushion pad
- long-arm stapler and staples

1 For the first cushion, slip-stitch the ends of a length of fringing, so that it doesn't unravel.

2 Cut a quarter circle from thin card and place it on the cushion as a guide for the curve of the fringing.

3 Slip-stitch along the edge of the fringing using a matching thread.

5 Slip-stitch the trimmings in place with matching thread.

7 Cut two equal squares of silver insulating material, large enough to fit the cushion pad and allowing for 4cm/ 1½in flat seam all around. Place the pad inside. Using a long-arm stapler, place one staple halfway along each side, to hold the cushion together.

4 Pin rows of black lace and fringing on to a yellow-ochre velvet cushion.

6 Stitch two parallel rows of black bobble trimming on to an orange silk cushion. First position one row and pin it in place, then use a tape measure to line up the second row accurately.

8 Beginning at one corner, staple all the way around the cushion 4cm/1½in from the edge.

FOUR-POSTER SARI

The drapes for this four-poster bed have been made from fine lengths of sari fabric. The sari lengths are made of silk, voile, organza and other fine fabrics that can be wrapped, folded and tucked without appearing at all bulky. Most saris are decorated with border designs and end pieces, with quite plain central areas. Try to visit a specialist sari shop where you will see a marvellous assortment of colours, embroideries, beadwork and patterns.

The saris used here are made from organza and the yellow and orange panels have been hung alternately around three sides of the bed.

Refer to the techniques section for how to make the four-poster frame.

YOU WILL NEED

- ◆ 8 sari lengths
- ◆ pins
- ◆ needle and matching sewing threads
- ◆ 15m/16½yd ribbon or braid
- ◆ scissors
- ◆ tape measure
- ◆ self-adhesive velcro dots (optional)
- ◆ 1 x 1m/1 x 1yd silk fabric
- ◆ square cushion pad
- ◆ tassels (optional)

2 Cut six 30cm/12in lengths of ribbon or braid per sari. These will be used as hanging loops.

1 Pin and then sew a length of ribbon or braid along the top of each sari. This will reinforce the fine fabric, so that the loops can be attached without puckering.

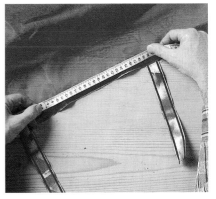

3 Arrange the ribbon lengths along the top of each sari, approximately 29cm/11½in apart.

4 Turn under one end of each ribbon and slip-stitch to the sari, leaving the other end loose. Hang the saris from the four-poster, looping the ribbons around the rail. Sew the loose ends with a few small slip-stitches, or use self-adhesive velcro dots. Peel off the backing and press the ribbon ends together as you hang the saris.

5 Place the cushion pad in the centre of the fabric.

6 Loosely fold two sides of the fabric over the cushion pad, then fold the other two sides over them. Slip-stitch the back seam but do not pull the fabric tightly around the cushion pad.

7 Turn the cushion over. Pull up the fabric in the centre and twist into a decorative knot.

8 Hold the knot in place with a few strategically placed stitches. Decorate with tassels if desired.

Above: The ribbon ties complement the braid on the edges of the saris.

ROPE-WRAPPED HEADBOARD

Quite apart from being one of the most stylish looks around, rope wrapping is a real pleasure to do. All you need is a frame, which can be a junk-shop find or a simple DIY structure made from construction timber. The wood is completely hidden by the coils of rope, so there is no need to prepare the surface in any way – just heat up the glue gun and get wrapping.

Rope comes in many different twists and thicknesses, some more decorative than others. Some ropes are made from natural fibres and others, like the one used here, are synthetic but resemble natural rope. One advantage of synthetic rope is that the cut ends can be sealed by holding them over a flame to melt the fibres together and prevent unravelling.

YOU WILL NEED

- ♦ rope
- ♦ wooden-framed headboard
- ♦ tape measure
- ♦ pen
- ♦ scissors or craft knife
- ♦ cutting mat or thick card
- ♦ lighter or matches (optional)
- ♦ glue gun and glue sticks

1 To calculate the length of rope needed to wrap each wooden post, first divide the height of the post by the thickness of the rope. Multiply this figure by the circumference of the post. Mark the rope at this point.

2 Cut the lengths of rope required to wrap all the posts. If you are using synthetic rope, seal the ends by holding them briefly over a flame to melt the fibres together.

3 Use the glue gun to stick the end of the rope to the back of the first post to be wrapped.

4 Wrap the rope tightly around the post, keeping the coils as close together as possible. If it helps to maintain the tension, apply a few dabs of hot glue to secure the rope as you go along.

5 Cut short lengths of rope to cover any gaps at intersections which cannot be wrapped. Insert the ends under the first coil of the intersecting post and glue in place.

6 Cut another length of rope to cover any loose ends and blobs of glue at the intersection. Glue the ends at the back of the post.

7 Make sure that all the intersections are finished in the same way so that the symmetry is maintained.

8 The wrapped headboard can be finished off with rope decorations. You could coil short lengths of rope into rhythmic swirls and glue them in place.

9 Alternatively, decorate the uprights with curls of rope. Pin the curves first, then glue into position. ----------▶

10 You could decorate the top rail with a row of crosses at the intersections and glue the ends of the crosses at the back.

Above: The rope details emphasize the mitred corners of the bedhead.

11 Or, a length of knotted rope along the top rail changes the outline of the bedhead. Tie a knot to go above each post, then glue in place.

CALICO TENT

Get that holiday feeling every morning when you look out on the day from your tent. This could make a novelty bedhead for a child's bedroom or a stylish feature in a contemporary adult's bedroom. The tent is made using a combination of fittings intended for different purposes. The chrome rods are shower rails, finished off in copper with plumber's pipe caps. The thin copper tube is also from the plumbing department – it has an attractive finish and can be bent easily with long-nosed pliers. The stability of the tent is assured by the use of shower rail sockets on the wall and a line of cup hooks on the ceiling. The fabric used here is unbleached calico, but you could use striped cotton duck or canvas if you prefer.

YOU WILL NEED

- ◆ 8 x 1m/8¾ x 1yd unbleached calico
- ◆ tape measure
- ◆ pencil
- ◆ ruler
- ◆ scissors
- ◆ 6m/6½yd iron-on hemming tape
- ◆ iron
- ◆ hacksaw
- ◆ 150cm/60in length of chrome shower rail
- ◆ centre punch
- ◆ hammer
- ◆ drill, with bit (the size of the copper tube)
- ◆ 1m/1yd narrow copper tube
- ◆ long-nosed pliers
- ◆ 3 chrome shower rail sockets
- ◆ spirit level
- ◆ screwdriver
- ◆ 6 chrome cup hooks and wall plugs
- ◆ 4m/4⅜yd white cord
- ◆ 3 copper pipe caps (to fit shower rail)

1 Decide upon the height of the top of the tent. Measure off the fabric and tear it to size.

2 Fold the fabric in four to find the centre and mark this point.

3 Measure 36cm/14in down each short edge and mark the points.

4 Draw a connecting line between the centre point and each of the side points. This will give the shape for the top of the tent.

5 Cut along the drawn lines, then cut a 3cm/1¼in notch at each of the points of the tent shape. Fold the fabric over to make a 3cm/1¼in seam around the top and sides of the fabric.

6 Use iron-on hemming tape to hold down the seams neatly. The two pieces should now meet at a right angle to make the tent shape. The sides and top of the tent will fold back to give a double thickness of fabric. Make three holes for the rails at the corner points and reinforce the fabric with an extra square of calico ironed on with hemming tape.

7 Use a hacksaw to cut the length of chrome shower rail into three 50cm/20in pieces.

8 Use a centre punch to dent the shower rail where the holes will be drilled, so that the drill does not slip. You will need to drill a hole 5cm/2in from one end of two of the poles and two holes in the other pole, the first 5cm/2in from one end and the second 1cm/½in in from it.

9 Drill the holes using a drill bit the same size as the copper tube. Use a hacksaw to cut two lengths of copper tube. Use the long-nosed pliers to bend one end of each copper tube into a hook shape. Use the chrome rail to estimate the curve of the hooks. Each hook should fit snugly around the chrome rail with its end fitting into the drilled hole.

10 Position the shower rail sockets on the wall so that the rails slot into them. Use a spirit level to check that the outer two are level.

11 Refer to the diagram below. Push the chrome rails through the holes in the back of the tent, then fit the copper tubes in place to hold the front section rigid. Fit the straight end of each copper tube into the hole in each side rail. Fit the hooked ends over the middle rail and into the two drilled holes. Fix a row of cup hooks to the ceiling directly above the front edge of the tent. Loop white cord around the cup hooks and the chrome rails for added stability. Finally, cap the chrome pipes with the copper caps.

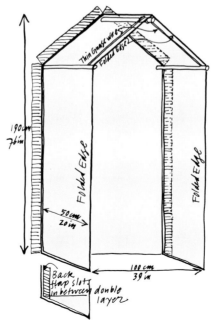

Above: The hooked copper tubes fit over and into the chrome rail. The cord is looped around the rail and crossed over to suspend the tent front from the cup hooks.

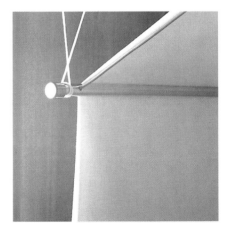

Above: The side rail is finished off with the copper cap and suspended from a crossed cord attached to the cup hooks.

HAMMOCK QUILT

It is only possible to relax and enjoy the sway of a hammock if you feel completely secure, so make quite sure that your wall fittings are sturdy and that the wall itself can take the strain. Use metal garage hooks with long screws and heavy-duty wall plugs. Once the safety angle has been covered, you can turn your attention to comfort and make a stylish no-sew quilt to dress up your hammock.

YOU WILL NEED

♦ iron

♦ 2.5m/2¾yd iron-on wadding

♦ 5m/5½yd blue fabric

♦ 2.5m/2¾yd black cotton fabric

♦ scissors

♦ tape measure

♦ iron-on hemming tape

♦ 5m/5½yd black iron-on mending tape

♦ pins

1 Iron the wadding to one half of the wrong side of the blue fabric. Fold the other half over so that the wadding is sandwiched between the fabric. Cut the black cotton fabric into 14cm/5½in strips. Iron down a 1cm/½in seam along the long edges. Iron each strip in half to make a long doubled strip 6cm/2¼in wide for the border. Place a length of iron-on hemming tape along each edge of the blue fabric and enclose each edge with a doubled black border strip. Iron to bond the fabrics together. Fold down the corners to achieve a mitred effect. Turn the fabric over and repeat the process on the other side.

2 Cut twenty-four 20cm/8in strips of black iron-on mending tape and use the tape measure to position them on the quilt in four rows of three crosses.

3 Pin the crosses in place if required, then iron them in position.

TARTAN BEDHEAD

Woollen tartan rugs are real comfort blankets, traditionally used on winter car journeys and picnics. The two rugs used in this project are doubled over, with their folded edges meeting in the middle. To complete the Highland hunting lodge atmosphere, the rugs are hung above the bedhead from a rough-hewn "branch".

YOU WILL NEED

- ◆ **2 matching tartan blankets or rugs**
- ◆ **tape measure**
- ◆ **needle and thick contrasting thread**
- ◆ **2.5cm/1in wooden dowel (slightly longer than the bed width)**
- ◆ **craft knife**
- ◆ **fine-grade sandpaper**
- ◆ **cloth**
- ◆ **shellac**
- ◆ **2 iron pipe holders (to fit 2.5cm/1in pipe)**
- ◆ **drill and wall plugs**
- ◆ **screwdriver**
- ◆ **kilt pins**

1 Fold each blanket in half lengthways and pin together along the folded seam. Blanket stitch the outside edges, then stitch the blankets together along the folded edge. If you don't like sewing, hold the seams closed with three kilt pins.

2 Start decorating the wooden pole by roughly carving away both ends of the dowel with a craft knife. Sand the rough edges with sandpaper. Use a cloth to rub shellac into the wood.

3 Fix the iron pipe holders to the wall using the drill and wall plugs, and a screwdriver. Fix the rail in place. Hang the blankets over the rail, with a 35cm/14in overlap to make a pelmet, pinning it in place with kilt pins.

MATERIALS

The materials used in these projects are many and varied, so look at the 'needs' list for your chosen project before you begin. The accompanying photograph shows a selection of most of the materials we have used.

The three most invaluable tools for this sort of work are a cordless electric drill; a glue gun and a staple gun. Staples are used for most upholstery work these days and a medium sized staple gun is ideal for drapes, pleats and upholstery. A cordless drill allows you the freedom of dashing up and down ladders and drilling in awkward places where there is no plug socket available. If you have never used a glue gun before, you will soon wonder how you managed without one — they can be used for glueing almost any two surfaces together and provide an instant bond that makes life a lot easier!

Iron-on hemming tape and mending tape are a great boon for those who don't sew. Follow the manufacturer's instructions but basically just run a length of tape between the two fabrics to be joined and heat with a hot iron. Sewing will be more time consuming but is more secure and long-lasting. Double sided carpet tape is very strong and a useful fixing for hemming heavy fabrics that are not going to be removed for washing.

Corrugated card (1); stencil card (2); iron-on hemming tape (3); tape measure (4); fabric paint (5); scissors (6); household paintbrush (7); square tipped artist's brushes (8); long nosed pliers (9); safety pins (10); pencil (11); stencil paint (12); water based paint (13); shellac (14); sand paper (15); glue gun (16); wire wool (17); webbing tape (18); blanket (19); staple gun (20); bias binding tape (21).

TECHNIQUES

You can buy DIY kits to make four-poster beds, but if you want to fit the structure around an existing bed it is less expensive to make it yourself. The lengths of timber between the posts are called stretchers.

YOU WILL NEED

♦ 4 lengths of 5 x 5cm/2 x 2in prepared soft wood, roughly door height (197cm/78in), for the posts

♦ 2 lengths of 5 x 2.5cm/2 x 1in prepared soft wood, mattress length plus 10cm/4in

♦ 2 lengths of 5 x 2.5cm/2 x 1in prepared soft wood, mattress width plus 10cm/4in

♦ 2 lengths of 15 x 2.5cm/6 x 1in prepared soft wood, mattress length plus 10cm/4in

♦ 2 lengths of 15 x 2.5cm/6 x 1in prepared soft wood, mattress width plus 10cm/4in

♦ drill

♦ mortice chisel

♦ saw

♦ wood glue

♦ 24 wood screws (countersunk)

♦ countersink bit

Making a four-poster bed

The ends of the timber stretchers are fitted into mortices in the posts. These are rectangular holes, cut to fit the insert. The posts are morticed on two sides at the top and again at mattress height. The mortices meet inside the timber at right angles. It may be possible to have these joints cut in the store or at a local carpenter's workshop, otherwise you can do it yourself by marking the shape of the insert on the post, drilling a series of holes, then chiselling out the shape.

1 Mitre the thinner timber stretchers by sawing the ends at a 45-degree angle. Apply a thin coating of wood glue to the mortices in one cornerpost.

Fit the first two mitred stretchers (one width, one length) into the mortices so the mitred ends meet inside and fit together comfortably. Support the other ends of the timbers as you do this, using a step ladder or an assistant.

2 Drill a hole on each outside surface of the post and screw in a countersunk screw to hold the timber stretchers firmly in place. Be aware of the position of the first screw when drilling for the second so that they do not cross. Repeat the process with the remaining stretchers.

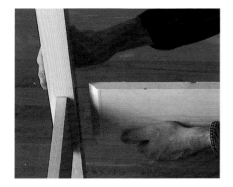

3 When all the top stretchers are in place, repeat steps 1 and 2 to fit the wider, lower stretchers.

Attaching a pole for a bedhead

1 To fit a wooden pole to the wall, first mark the positions for drilling the holes by holding each pipe fitting in position and using a pencil to mark the wall. Slide the pole through the fitting. Drill and plug the holes, then screw the pipe fittings into the wall.

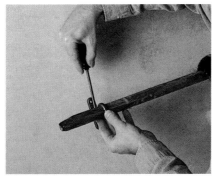

2 Pipe fittings like this one have an adjustable split ring that is tightened from above. Use a screwdriver to adjust the fittings so that the pole is held firmly in place.

Hospital corners

1 Tuck the sheet and blanket under the mattress at the end of the bed.

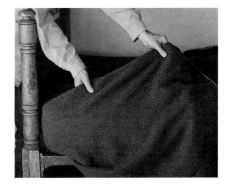

2 Pull up the side edge firmly, so that the excess blanket is flattened into a neat triangular shape.

3 Place one hand flat against the side of the mattress to hold this folded section in place. Pull the side edge of the blanket down and over. Slide your hand out and firmly tuck the blanket and sheet under the mattress. It should look like a neat mitred corner.

TEMPLATES

A E O

L M R

ACKNOWLEDGEMENTS

The authors and publishers would like to thank the following for generously supplying materials used in this book:

After Noah
121 Upper Street
London N1 1QP
(metal bedsteads, children's toys, shaker peg rail and furniture, and accessories)

Damask Bed Linen
Unit 10
Sulivan Enterprise Centre
Sulivan Road
London SW6 3BS
(all bed linen, and paisley quilt)

Picture credits
p8 Steve Tanner; **p9** *bottom* Simon Brown/Options IPC Magazines/ Robert Harding Syndication; **p10** James Duncan; **p11** *bottom* Polly Wreford/Country Homes and Interiors/Robert Harding Syndication; **p13** Schulenburg/The Interior Archive; **p15** *left* Tom Leighton/ Homes and Gardens/Robert Harding Syndication; **p15** *right* Schulenburg/ The Interior Archive; **p16** Simon Brown/The Interior Archive; **p16** *left* Schulenburg/ The Interior Archive; **p16** *right* Ari Ashley/The Interior Archive.

Early's of Witney PLC
Household Textiles Division
Witney Mill
Witney, Oxfordshire
OX8 5EB
(wool blankets)

Special thanks to Sacha Cohen, Josh George and Sarah Pullin for all their hard work in the studio.

INDEX